Let's Create Faith A Pet!

Joy

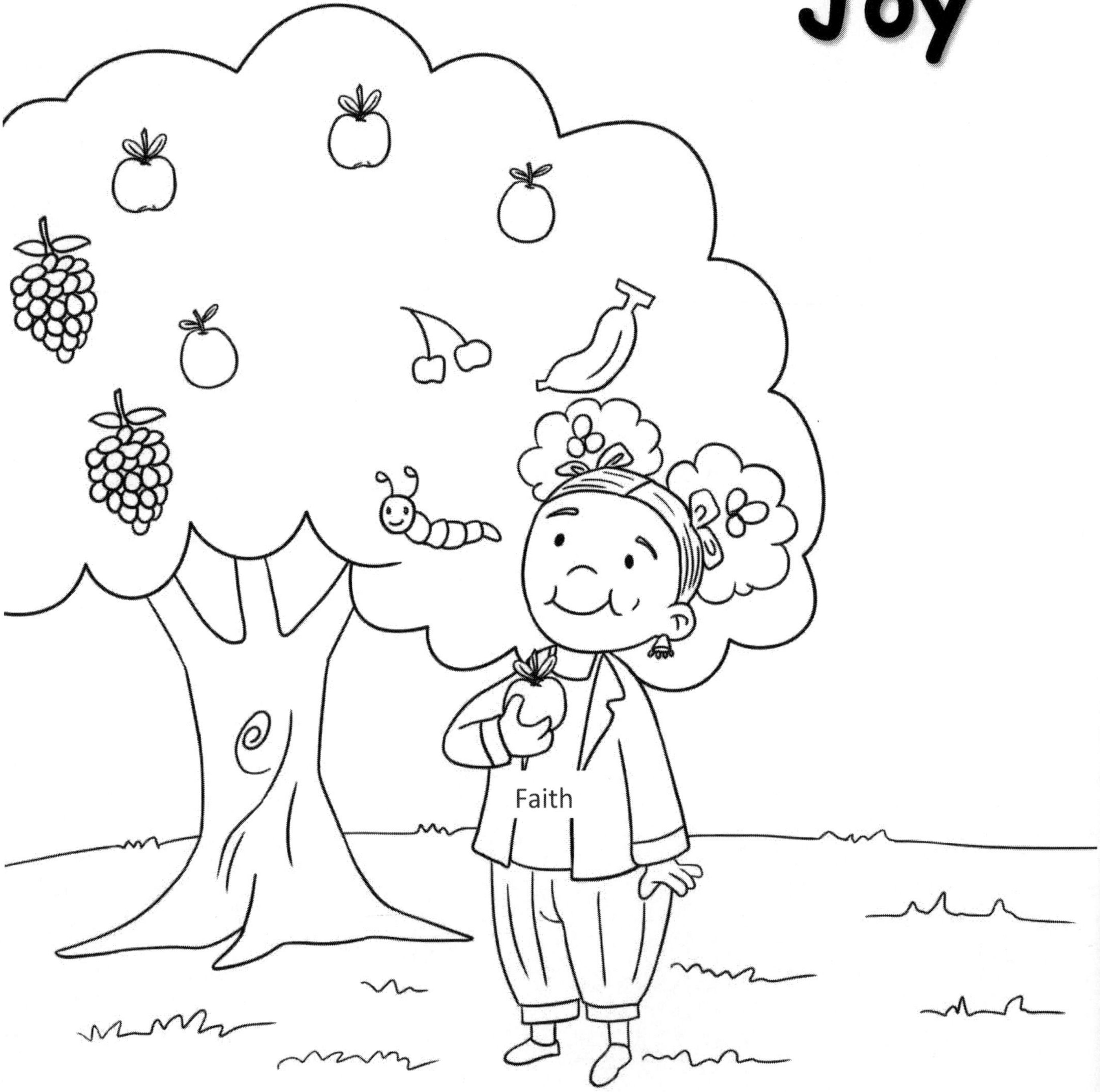

Gentleness

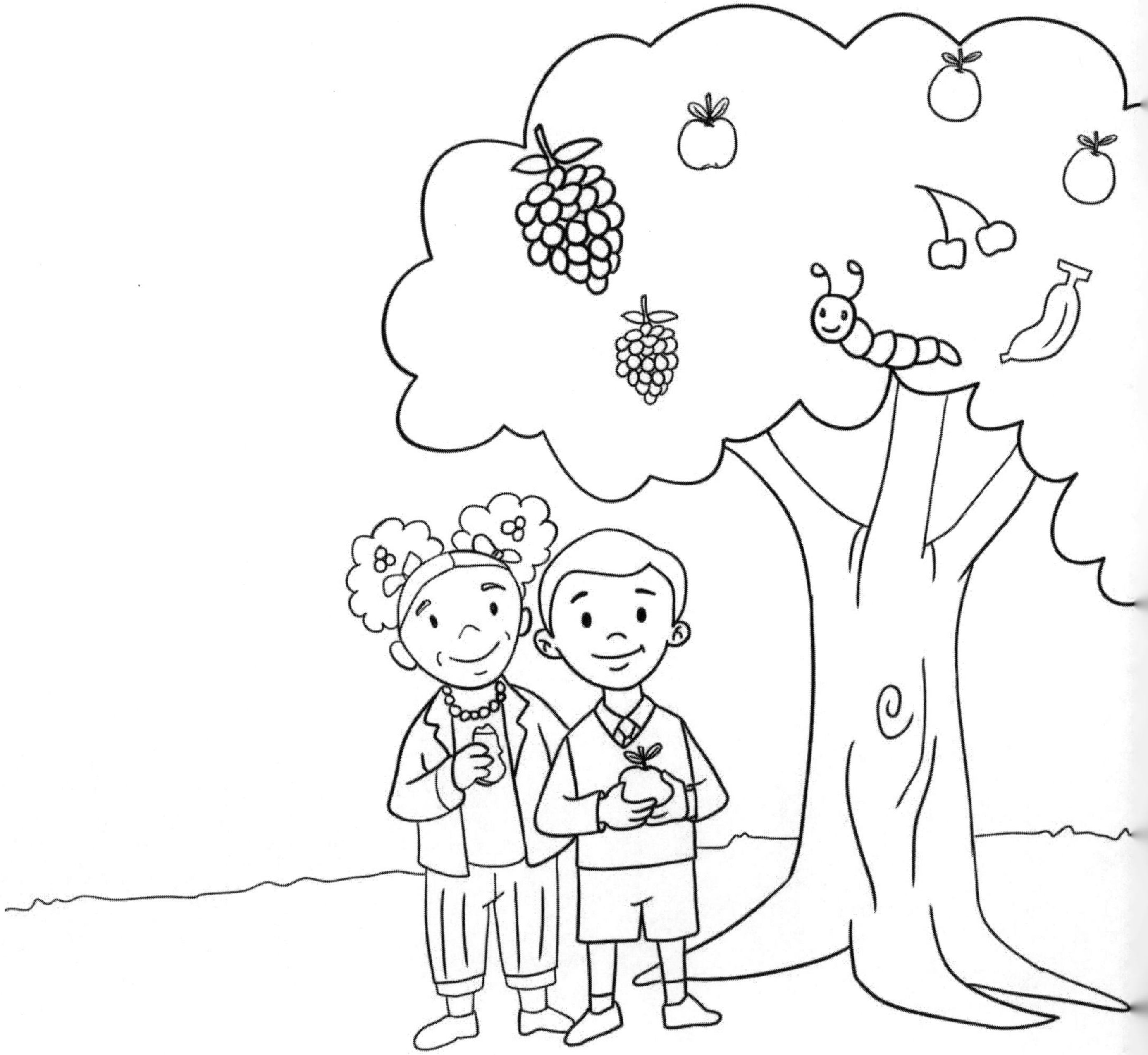

Patience

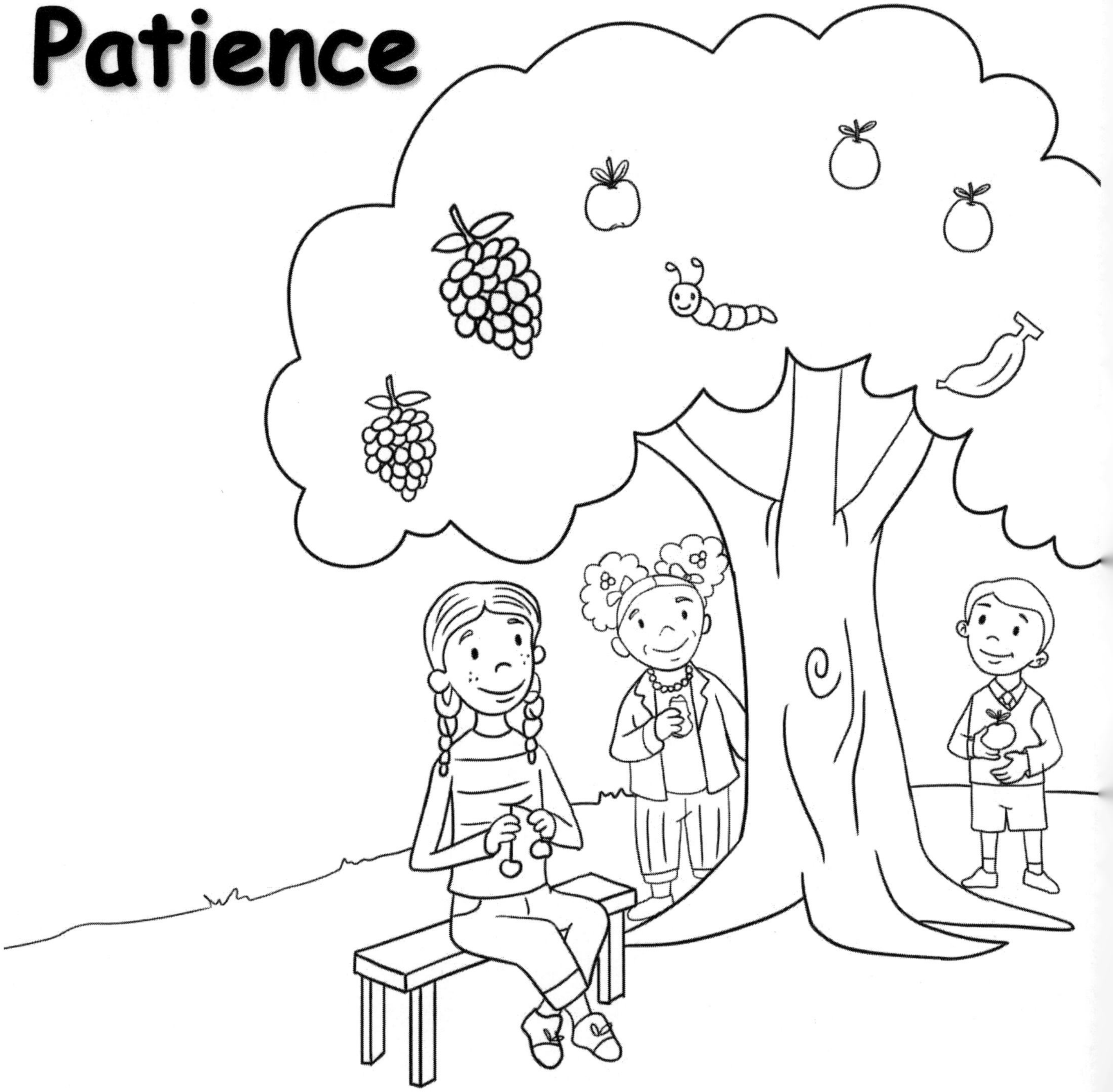

Self-Control

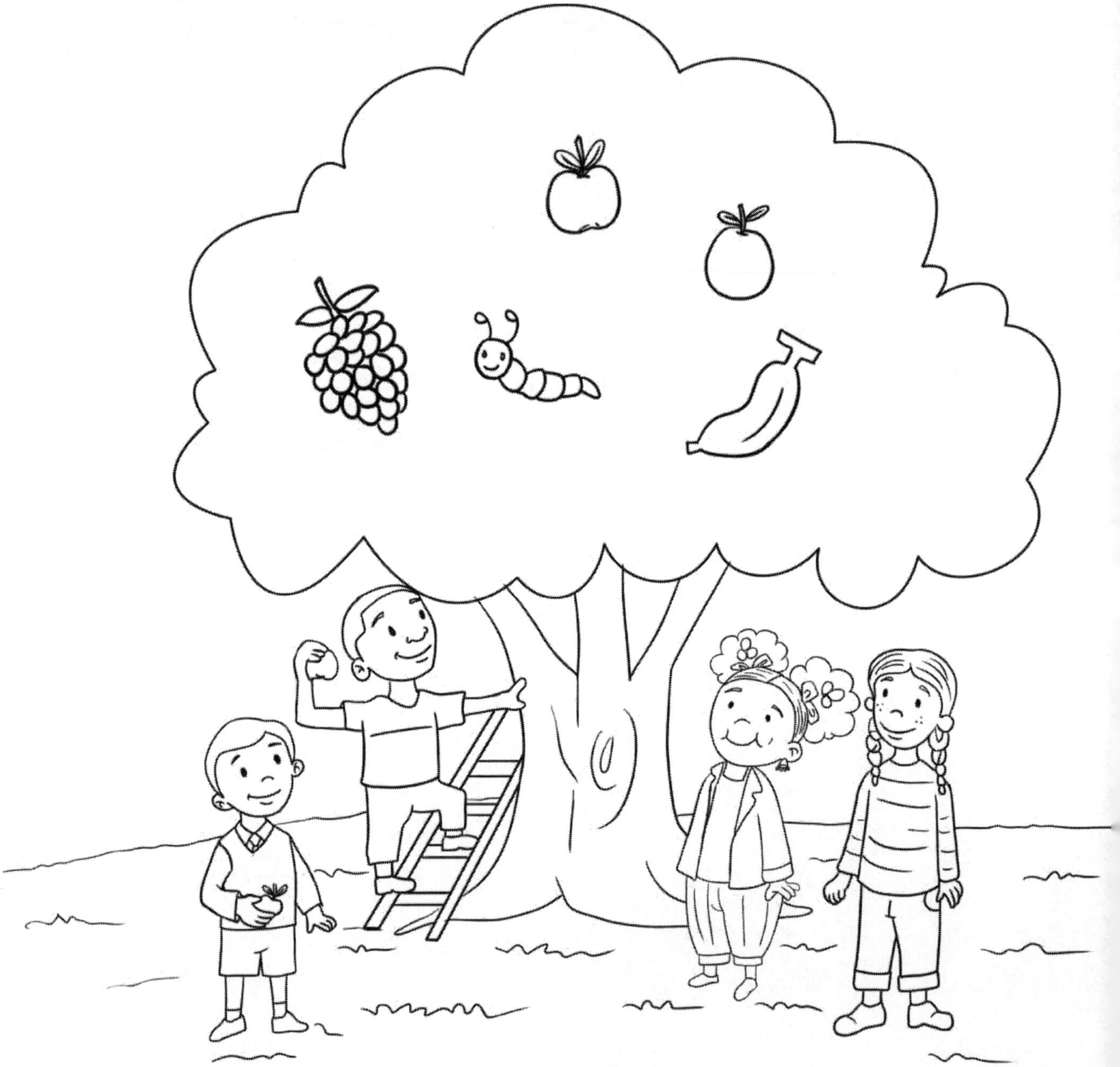

Sharing

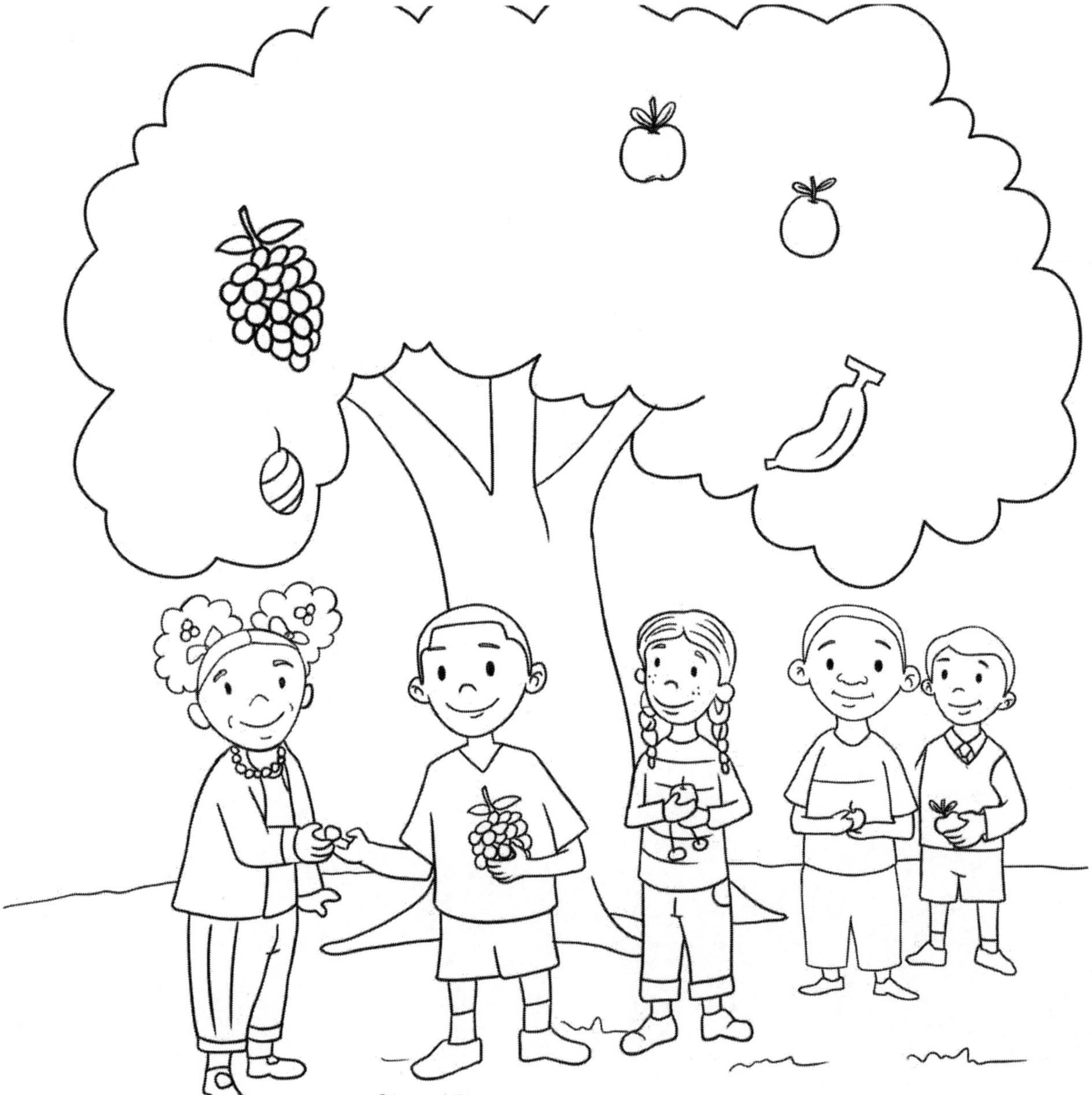

Goodness

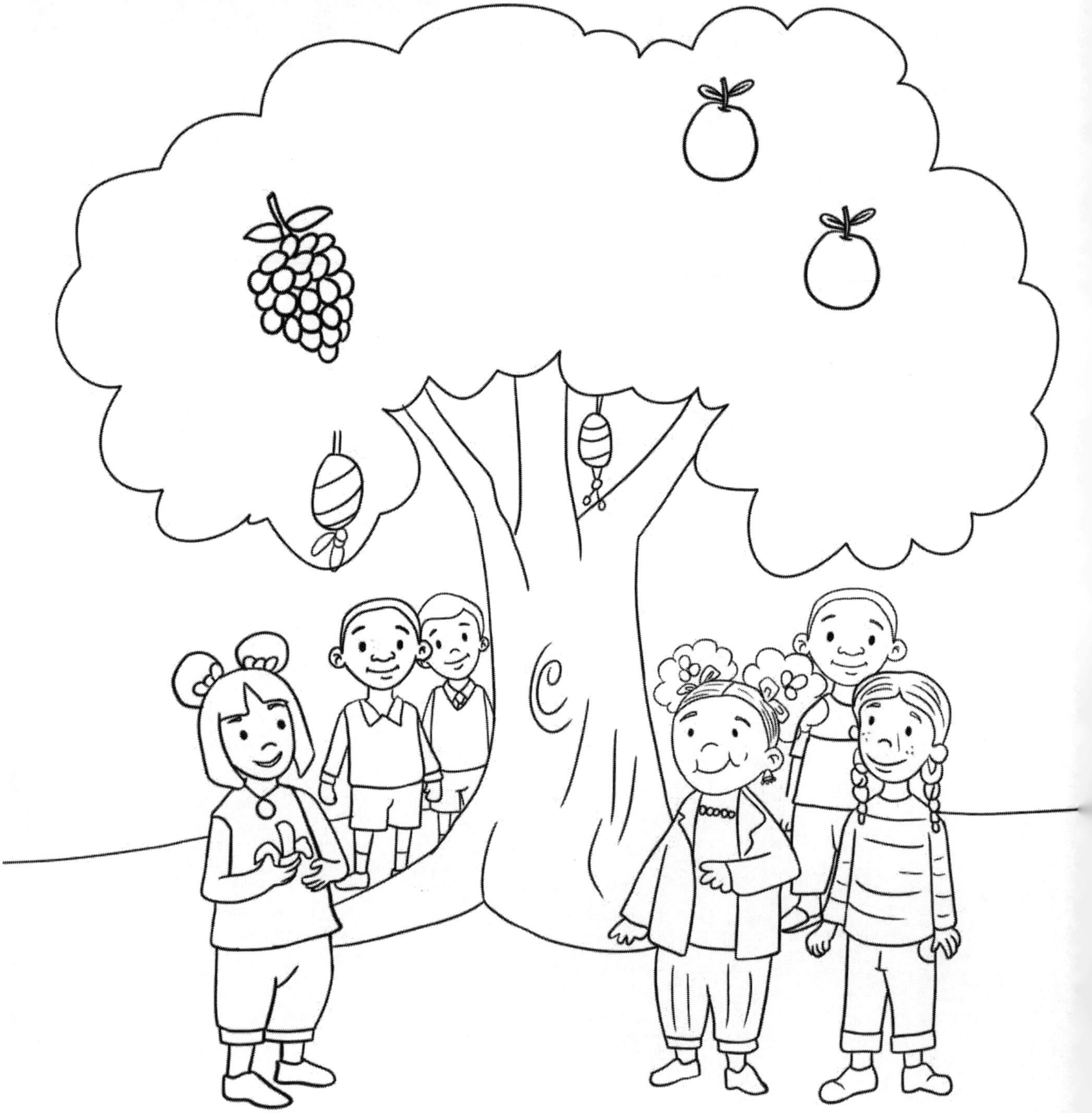

Peace

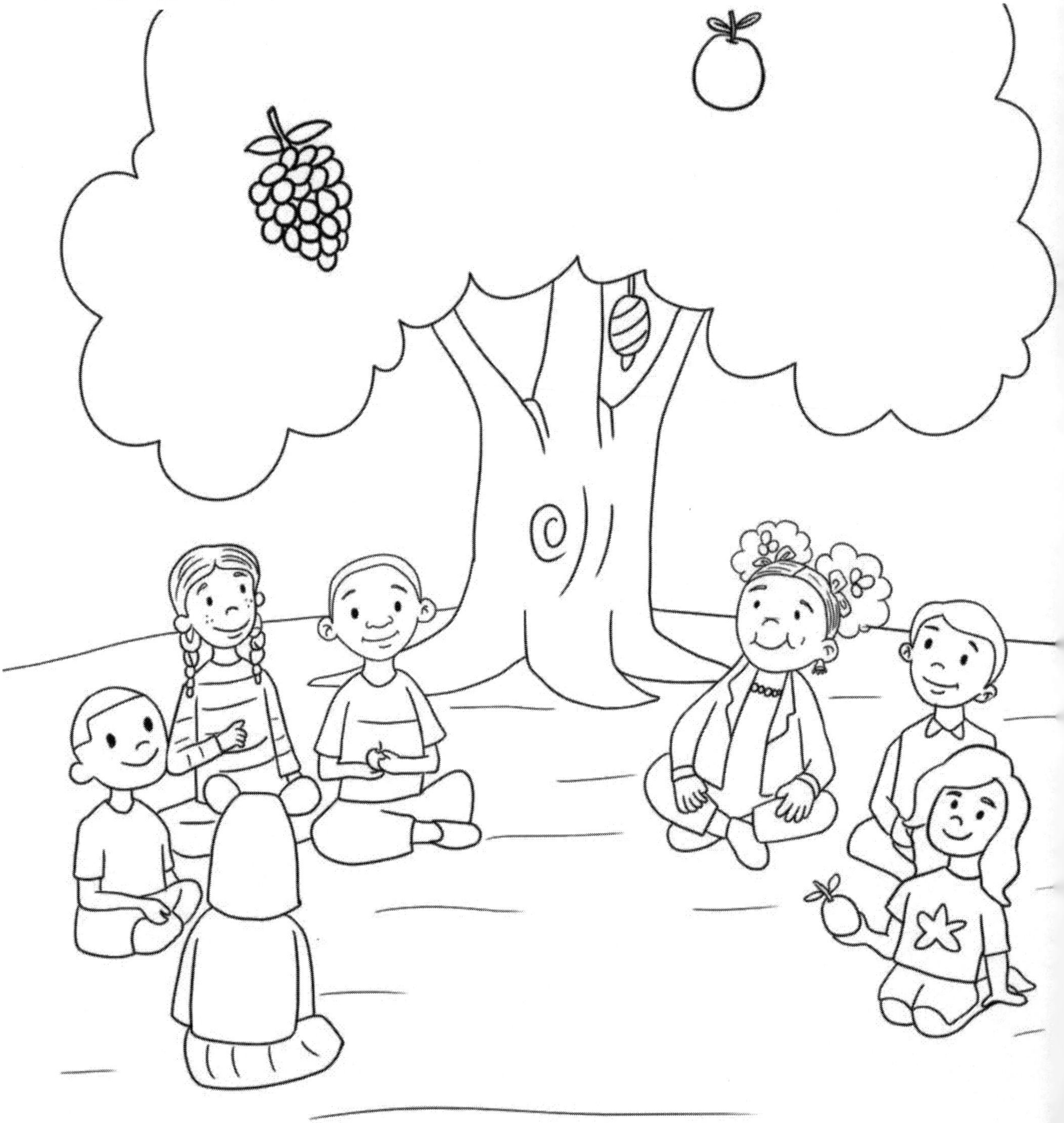

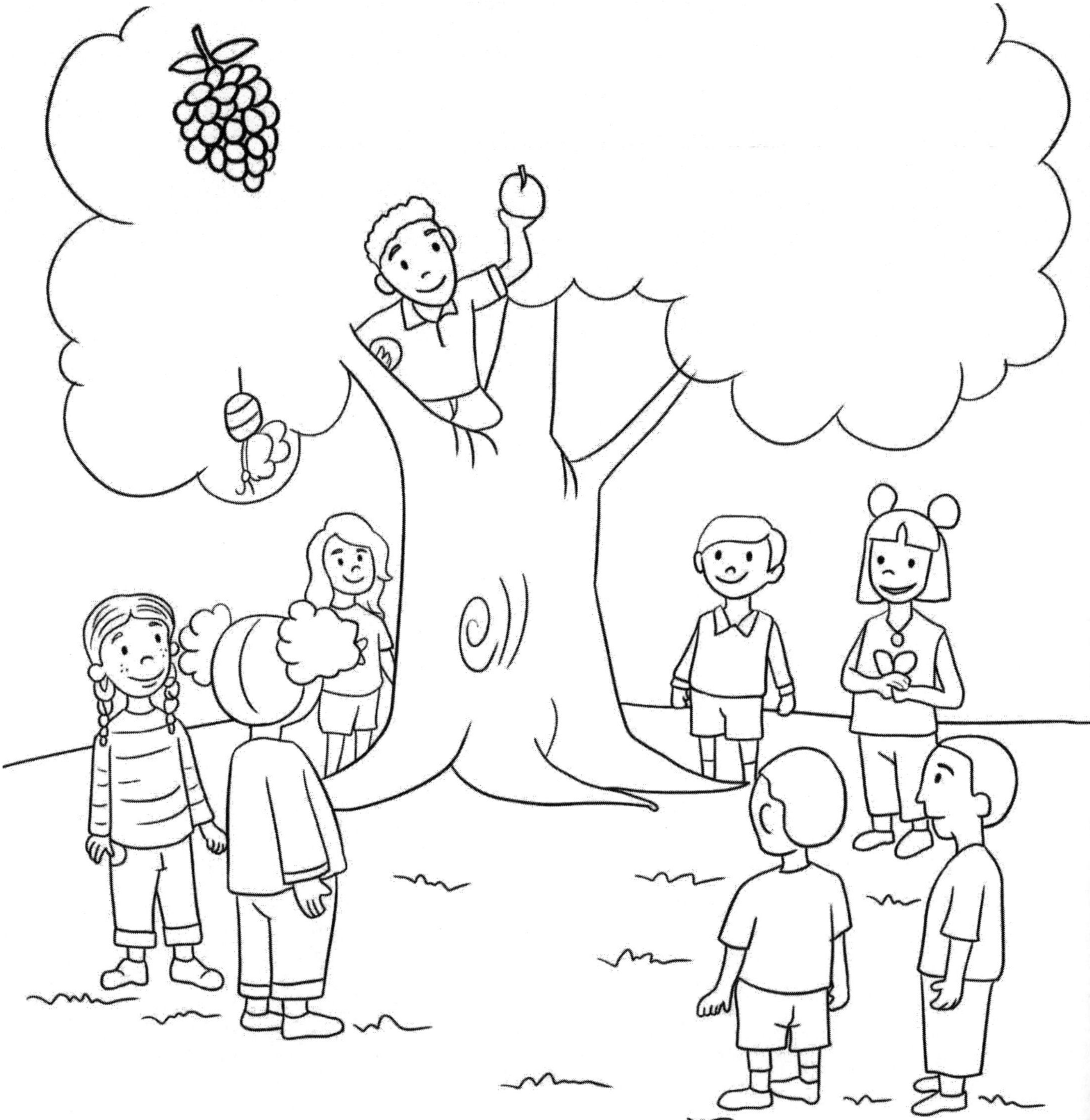

Believe

Love

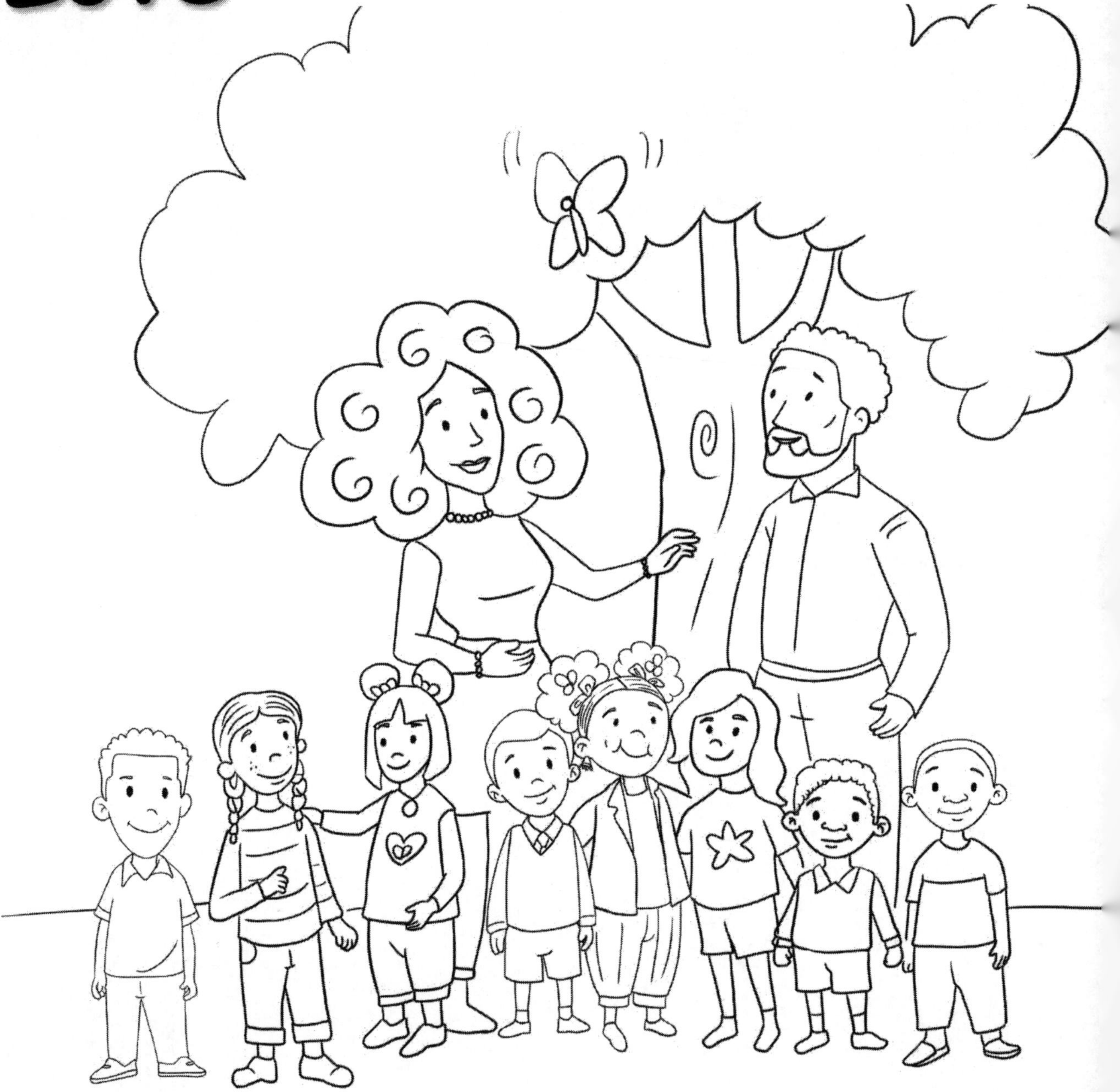

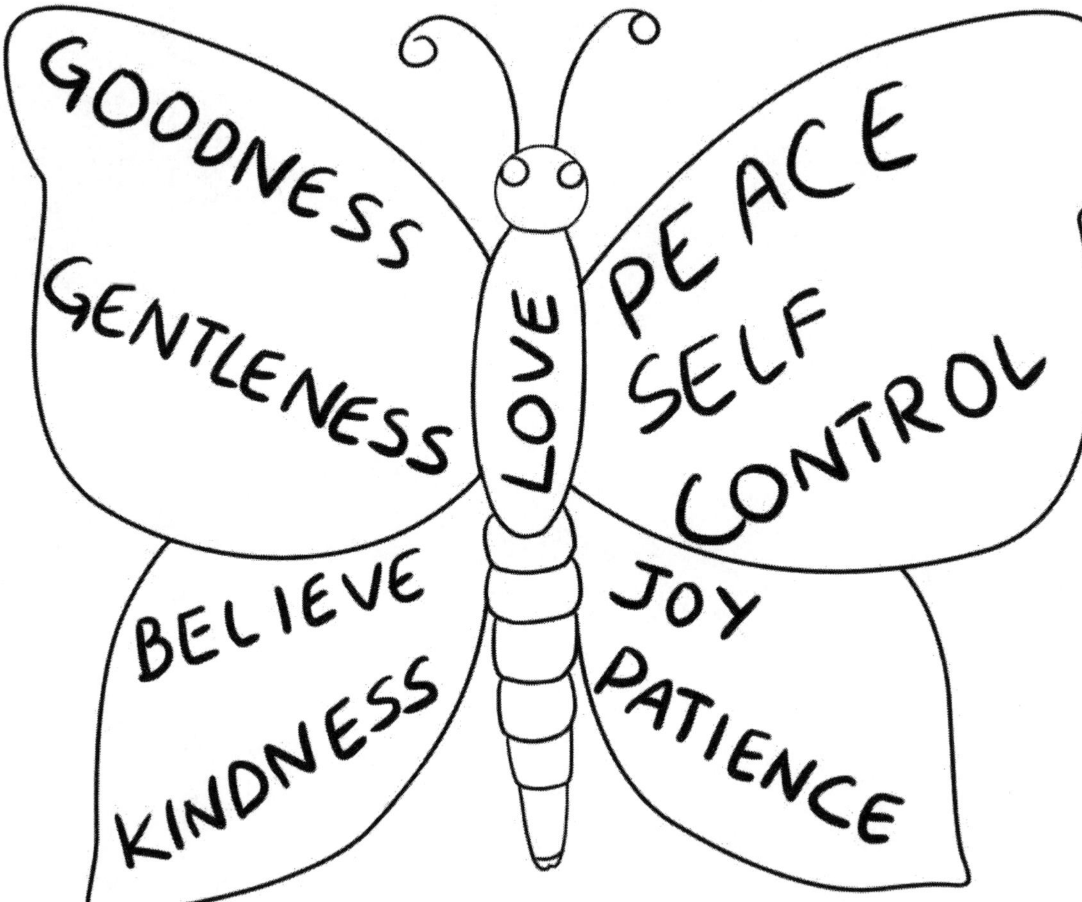
GOODNESS
GENTLENESS
LOVE
PEACE
SELF CONTROL
BELIEVE
KINDNESS
JOY
PATIENCE

Made in the USA
Columbia, SC
15 August 2023

21685708R00015